Towards a New Nigeria

TOWARDS A
NEW NIGERIA

A Framework for Its Future

Obinna Izeogu

This book was conceptualized, designed, and published by Obinna Izeogu in New Jersey, The United States. The book was typeset and made into pages by Obinna Izeogu in Adobe InDesign.

Towards a New Nigeria: A Framework for Its Future
by Obinna Izeogu

Copyright © 2019, 2022 by Obinna Izeogu

All rights reserved. No portion of this book may be reproduced in any form without permission from the publisher, except as permitted by U.S. copyright law.
For permissions contact: obinna.izeogu@gmail.com

ISBN 979-8-9867261-0-6

*For my unborn child in the womb
and all children of African descent.
May you go on to serve your communities
by bringing prosperity through the work
of your intellect.*

Contents

Foreword   09

01 The Challenges Faced By Nigeria   15

02 Learning From The International Community   27

03 The Stakeholders   37

04 Principles for Sustainability   45

05 Systems Thinking for Systemic Problems   49

06 Life-Cycle Analysis   57

07 Collective Intelligence   63

08 Framework   79

References   83

And I believe that the best learning process of any kind of craft is just to look at the work of others.
　　　Wole Soyinka

If you define the goal of a society as GNP, that society will do its best to produce GNP. It will not produce welfare, equity, justice, or efficiency unless you define a goal and regularly measure and report the state of welfare, equity, justice, or efficiency.
　　　Donella H. Meadows

A large part of mathematics which becomes useful developed with absolutely no desire to be useful, and in a situation where nobody could possibly know in what area it would become useful; and there were no general indications that it ever would be so.
　　　John von Neumann, Address to Princeton Alumni, 1954

I think the history of science has shown that valuable consequences often proliferate from simple curiosity.
　　　Claude Shannon

Foreword

When I began writing this book, I was consumed with a singular thought: create innovation in the way public policy is perceived in Nigeria. I was inspired by the burgeoning Afrobeats scene. I wanted to make civic life and the debates about it that ensued cool. I wanted to give it the same presence of a Burna Boy music video consumed avidly by fans globally. The millions of views are seen as the pride of Nigeria, the confidence of an African on the world stage. The vibrancy of the comments section in a YouTube video of Burna like "Ye". The viral reach of his mom, Mama Burna, who declared the sacrosanct unity of Africa and the diaspora in a speech receiving an award in the place of her son. At least this is where I started, this is the appearance I intended to project to Nigeria. I viewed it as existing within the realm of the possible even in the face of the impossible.

How does one make public policy innovative? How does one write about it with the earnestness to deliver creative ideas that spring from the curiosity to redirect a country facing strong headwinds with the use of mental instruments? More than an intellectual exercise, the book is personal. I grew up in Nigeria reciting its national anthem in primary school. I belted out:

Arise, O Compatriots, Nigeria's call obey
To serve our Fatherland
With love and strength and faith.
The labour of our heroes past
Shall never be in vain...

So even though I now live in The United States, I care deeply about my Fatherland. It is the most populous Black country in the world. It is the most populous African country. It is a country with deep roots extending to the diaspora. Nigeria is important. Nigeria must not fail.

It is with this spirit in mind that I found my motivation to use all my mental instruments to create this book: *Towards a New Nigeria*. The title for the book gives a nod to Le Corbusier's *Towards a New Architecture*, an influential book that helped to transform the built environment in the 20th century. I want this book to have the same impact on the discourse on civic life for Nigerians. I want it to be a utopian vision for civic innovation in the lives of Nigerians, for Nigeria.

My thinking ever since I went to university in New York state has been influenced by design. I studied its theories; its propositions that attempt to prove that everything is designed in some way or another. By extension, as designers, we are capable of designing everything from "a spoon to the city". It is the modernist ideal. We do live today in a post-modernist world informed by the culture wars, memes, identity politics, and late-stage capitalism amongst other conceptualizations that seek to show the break from the world created by the modernists. These Other theories have also been influential in my intellectual development. For me, the link between modernism and post-modernism has been the crucial role played by cybernetics.

In writing this book, I took the approach of a design engineer crafting civic policy as an innovation framework. Processes for creating solution instruments began with research and design: identifying needs through problem framing; collecting information by researching what already exists; thinking about the stakeholders: what do they want? And who wants it? Operational research and planning through determining what's realistic and limiting. Conducting hazard analyses that define what can go wrong; specifications for a policy that determine what's required; foregrounding conceptual design by showcasing potential solutions; finally, prototype design by envisioning a preferred design. This essentially makes up the innovation approach.

Without bringing together different elements from diverse disciplines, I don't think I could have reached the conclusions I've drawn from research and potentially positioning the framework of a civic innovation platform that references everything from Taguchi methods to the swarm intelligence of a network similar to the immune system in its complexity and ability to solve complex problems. Ultimately, Nigeria's problems are systemic and complex. I hope this book begins to put on the table, not just the problems faced by Nigeria, but a yet-to-be-imagined existence that transforms its environment, economy, and society. Thus, creating a new Nigeria. An imagined future of civic innovation. I'd like to believe this is possible. Can civic life use the framework of a networked society to engage in fruitful policy design with a bottom-up approach? We see the power of coordination, cooperation, collaboration, and deliberation work so well for insects like ants when faced with complex problems in the environment. We observe their emergent behavior. Robot swarms, too, use this logic designed by A.I. researchers. Can policy innovation in Nigeria happen through collective intelligence? These are some of the propositions yet to be proved. Let's see where they get us in terms of mental instruments designed to tackle the problems Nigeria faces.

Obinna Izeogu

01
The Challenges Faced By Nigeria

Poverty

The Nigerian economy is the largest in Africa. In 2017, the country had a nominal GDP of $376.3 billion. It came out ahead of both South Africa ($349.3 billion) and Egypt ($237 billion) ranked second and third, respectively. Nigeria's economy has grown in recent years, yet one of the central challenges facing its development and sustainable growth is poverty. According to Yemi Kale, the head of Nigeria's Bureau of Statistics, "despite the fact that the Nigerian economy is growing, the proportion of Nigerians living in poverty is increasing every year." According to The Borgen Project, citizens living in absolute poverty has risen 12.3% from 54.7% in 2004 (Bramlett, 2018).

The Economy

The high unemployment rate strikes at the core of the Nigerian economy. According to The World Bank, it contributes to "high poverty levels, of regional inequality, and of social and political unrest in the country" (The World Bank, 2018). An economy tethered solely to the fluctuations of global oil and gas prices exacerbates the situation. Nigeria needs to face the challenges of diversification of its economy, "insufficient infrastructure, building strong and effective institutions, as well as governance issues, public financial management systems, human development indicators, and the living conditions of the population" to drive growth and development (The World Bank, 2018). Indices, benchmarks, and key metrics help as reference points—for example, set points in control theory—to steer the inputs of the country toward the output of desired outcomes.

The Human Development Index (HDI) acts as a set point which can be applied as feedback for corrective action. The HDI is a statistic composite index of life expectancy, education, and per capita income indicators. It is used to rank countries into tiers of human development: life expectancy at birth, knowledge and education, standard of living. The World Bank writes, "Nigeria has made significant progress in socio-economic terms over the last 15 years. Between 2005 and 2015, Nigeria's Human Development Index value increased by 13.1%" (The World Bank, 2018).However, Nigeria ranks at 157 according to the UNDP (United Nations Development Programme). For comparison, South Africa ranks at 113.

Gender Equality

Archaic attitudes toward gender prevail in the society at large. Many still hold beliefs and attitudes maintaining patriarchal institutions. For example, people still believe that only men should occupy positions of power in political offices, professions, and business. Consequently, women in Nigeria have limited opportunities in shaping and contributing fully to the actualization of the country's full potential. Unemployment is high among women. They face discrimination and violence (Mike, 2018). Their exclusion from full participation in social, political, and economic life is detrimental to the country's future.

Poor Standard of Education

Nigeria holds the unenviable position of having the largest population of out-of-school learning youth in the world. Professor Hassana Alidou, UNESCO (United Nations Education, Scientific, and Cultural Organisation) country director in Nigeria, signaled in the Education For All (EFA) Global Monitoring Report (GMR) a high level of gender inequality and inequity in some parts of Nigeria. The report indicates the prohibitive cost of education in the country. The Dakar Framework For Action (EFA - Education For All), agreed to by 164 governments worldwide with participation from Nigeria with six goals of Education for All, adopted in Dakar in 2000 by 2015. The framework for government addresses "the basic, transferable and technical skills of the youth, as well as the challenges of access, equity, quality, gender and poverty trap" (Premium Times Nigeria, 2018). Minister of Education, Professor Ruqayyatu Ahmed Rufa'i, called on the country to relinquish the stigma associated with Technical and Vocational Education and Training (TVET). She remarks on the impact the negative public perception has on efforts being made to revitalize the sector.

At the university level, there is rampant corruption by both students and faculty. Professors are known to request and take money for good grades (Mike, 2018). Nigeria's Independent Corrupt Practices and Other Related Offences Commission reports in 2014 on the endemic corruption of Nigerian universities due to a lack of accountability and persistent failure of the enforcement of standards. In the ICPC's "University System Study Review, Professor Olu Aina, said there was a lack of 'political will' to deal with corruption violations, few internal checks, and balances in universities to prevent corruption and little external oversight of corrupt practices" (Mike, 2018).

Unemployment

From 1991 to 2017, The World Bank indicates that the average unemployment value for Nigeria during that period was 4.53% with a minimum of 3.7% in 2013 and a maximum of 7.06% in 2016. Unemployment remains high for youth at an average of 9.94%. Overall labor force participation was at an average of 55.28%. That value is lower for women. They have an average of 43.58% participation in the labor force (The Global Economy, 2018). Some argue that the values might actually be more severe. As Mike writes: "Unemployment is a hot issue in Nigeria, and many people are frustrated with widespread joblessness. Unemployment in Nigeria is like a disease that the cure is [sic] not yet discovered" (Mike, 2018).

Health and Human Services

For several years, Nigeria has suffered from a deteriorating health sector. More recently it became a major area of concern for the Nigerian government. The two pronged issue of

population control and increased life expectancy are seen as
essentially compatible programmes in Nigeria. As the
National Planning Commissions reports, "Government must rely
on adequate health statistics for planning and monitoring its
relevant programmes" (National Planning Commissions, n.d.).

Prior to independence from colonial rule, data on health were
collected by the respective regional governments' departments
of health. National Planning Commissions reports: "Data were
[sic] obtained from the few general hospitals, infectious diseases
hospitals and public health units. Initially, emphasis was on
keeping records of reported cases of, and deaths from, communicable diseases such as small pox, cholera, malaria, tuberculosis,
leprosy and yaws. Records of immunisation were also kept.
Administrative records of health resources, manpower and vital
statistics were among the earliest items of data kept by the regional departments of health" (National Planning Commissions, n.d.).

There are several examples which show that health statistics contributed to advances in medicine. Those advances would not have
been possible without health statistics, "especially those generated on longitudinal basis" (National Planning Commissions, n.d.).

A research report by the Nigeria Centre For Disease Control
asserts the requirement for "robust public health infrastructures"
(Barzilay et al., 2018). The researchers mention the dependence of
health security on "systems that promote, maintain, and
restore health." They go on to write: "Health systems are
stronger and more effective with integrated core functions of

public health, including but not limited to surveillance of population health and well-being; monitoring and response to health hazards and emergencies; advancing public health research to develop the evidence to inform policies and programs; and assuring a sufficient and competent public health workforce" (Barzilay et al., 2018). Health research data and epidemiologic data ensure the provision of an "evidence base" for decision making affecting "all aspects of the larger health system" (Barzilay et al., 2018). Nigeria has suffered from the loss of talent through successive cycles of "brain drain". As the report notes, "a strong public health workforce increases the capacity of a country to ensure the existence of the conditions in which people can be healthy" (Barzilay, 2018).

Crime and Terrorism

The perception of Nigeria as a haven for criminality is held by both its citizens and other countries. Rampant crime such as kidnapping and trafficking afflict the nation. The rise in criminal behavior can be linked to unemployment and other factors associated with hopelessness unduly felt by some relegated to the fringe of civil society. Their behavior is a response to the lack of opportunities and self realization constructive to not only their own development, but also that of their country.

Terrorism and insecurity cripple the nation. Boko Haram, a moniker meaning "Western" or "non-Islamic" education is a sin, has the goal of replacing the Nigerian Government with an

Islamic state ruled by strict sharia law. It ultimately has the objective of establishing an Islamic caliphate throughout Africa. According to the CIA (Central Intelligence Agency), the terrorist group aims to "destroy any political or social activity associated with Western society; conducts attacks against primarily civilian and regional military targets" (CIA, 2018). With headquarters in the northeast of Nigeria, the group have killed tens of thousands of Nigerians during hundreds of attacks and disrupted the regional economy of trade and farming. These activities have put the region at risk of famine and the displacement of millions of people. The CIA goes on to note the group's violent opposition to any form of political or social activity associated with societies of the West. This includes: attending secular schools, and wearing Western dress (CIA, 2018). ISIS West Africa (Islamic State of Iraq and ash-Sham) also hampers the country's security: "with its largest presence in the northeast and the Lake Chad region; targets primarily regional military installations and civilians" (CIA, 2018).

Corruption

For several decades, Nigeria has been suffering from the scourge of corruption. However, The Economic and Financial Crimes Commission (EFCC) Act (2004) is a step in the right direction with the establishment of legislation and judicial prosecution: the right to hold or dispose of property (whether moveable [sic] or immovable) and be the designated Financial Intelligence Unit (FIU) in Nigeria, "which is charged with the responsibility of coordinating the various institutions involved in the fight against money laundering and enforcement of all laws dealing with economic and financial crimes in Nigeria" (EFCC, 2004). The EFCC reports on its website a total of "312 convictions in 2018" stated by Ibrahim Magu, acting Chairman, EFCC. He goes on to say: "The Commission is committed to intensifying its efforts in order to ensure that it secures more convictions in 2019" (EFCC, 2019). The EFCC endeavors to cooperate internationally. Financial crime is global. To properly tackle financial crime, the European Union has pledged support and funding through the 9th European Development Fund with further assistance on implementation by the United Nations Office on Drugs and Crime (UNODC). These collaborations are meant to intervene through: "the strengthening of the operational capacities of the agency, including the provision of specialized training for staff and management, the delivery of basic operational equipment, the building of the EFCC's Training and Research Institute, as well as the creation of a forensic laboratory and the mentoring of its staff" (EFCC, n.d).

The Environment

As an oil producing nation, Nigeria faces environmental challenges that go back decades. Its fossil fuel industry, dirty energy, has polluted the very areas responsible for the majority of the revenue coming into the country. Local economies and ecologies have been, and continue to be, devastated by the disregard for environmental accountability at the governmental and corporate level. Ken Saro-Wiwa, a prominent Nigerian environmental activist and writer, was executed in 1995 because he took a stand for environmentalism in Ogoniland.

On the other hand, Nigeria has signed most of the international agreements and protocols for creating a sustainable environment (Okeke, 2018); for example, the United Nations Sustainable Development Goals (SDGs). However, execution and implementation is a challenge to Nigeria and other Sub-Saharan African countries (Okeke, 2018). One of the egregious examples of environmental catastrophe in Nigeria is Ogoniland and the oil spills that have wrecked the community, depriving local residents of sustenance and livelihood because of extreme pollution. The remediation, according to Okeke, has been slow with little progress to show for the endeavor. UNDP (United Nations Development Programme) reports findings from its analysis of the community:

- Soil contamination from oil spills
- Groundwater contamination from oil spills
- Surface water and sediment contamination in the creeks.
- Adverse impacts on ecosystems (flora and fauna) due to oil field infrastructure and activities (United Nations Environment Programme, 2007)

Unlike Rwanda, Nigeria is yet to phase out or ban polythene bags. The environmental pollution is there for all to see. Okeke reports: the government has made several pronouncements; however, action is yet to be seen. Polythene litters the environment. Found in little nooks and crannies, in bodies of water becoming "an environmental nuisance and a hazard" (Okeke, 2018).

Sanitation and waste management continue to bedevil the Federal Ministry of Environment. Several waste management projects were started a few years ago; however, they did not stand the test of time (Okeke, 2018).

Okeke makes mention of other environmental challenges such as flooding, clean energy, and the great green wall (Okeke, 2018). The latter addresses the displacement of millions of people through desertification and the destruction of lives and property in the former. On clean energy, Okeke writes: "Despite Nigeria's huge clean energy potentials, a majority of Nigerian households still rely on firewood and solid biomass for cooking" (Okeke, 2018).

02
Learning From The International Community

The 2030 Agenda for Sustainable Development

Adopted by all Member States in 2015, The 2030 Agenda for Sustainable Development provides a framework to attain peace and prosperity for all people around the world and the planet, both now and into the future. The core of the blueprint are the 17 Sustainable Development Goals (SDGs): an immediate call to action for both developed and developing countries— indeed all countries—to form a global partnership. As the UN writes on its SDGs Knowledge Platform about Member States:

> They recognize that ending poverty and other deprivations must go hand-in-hand with strategies that improve health and education, reduce inequality, and spur economic growth—all while tackling climate change and working to preserve our oceans and forests (Sustainable Development Goals, n.d.).

Several decades of work by both countries and the UN Department of Economic and Social Affairs occurred: from Agenda 21 at The Earth Summit in Rio de Janeiro, Brazil in 1992 with more than 178 countries adopting the agenda to Transforming Our World to The 2030 Agenda for Sustainable Development in New York in September 2015 which had the 17 SDGs and their related thematic issues such as water, energy, climate, oceans, urbanization, transport, science and technology (Sustainable Development Goals, n.d.).

The European Manifesto

On 17 December 2012, the European Commission circulated a memo titled: Manifesto For A Resource-Efficient Europe. The document outlines a strategy for abandoning the linear process of "take, make, waste" and moving toward a regenerative circular economy which is also resource-efficient. The memo puts forth a stark position: Europe has no choice (European Commission, 2012).

The future of Europe and its economy, its competitiveness depends on its ability "to get more added value, and achieve overall decoupling, through a systemic change in the use and recovery of resources in the economy" (European Commission, 2012).

Against the backdrop of Rio+20 Summit (The United Nations Conference on Sustainable Development in Rio de Janeiro, Brazil in 2012), The European Resource Efficiency Platform was created as a call to action for business, labor and civil society leaders to encourage and support resource efficiency and "the transformation to a circular economy and society now because this offers a path out of the current crisis towards a reindustrialisation of the European economy on the basis of resource-efficient growth that will last" (European Commission, 2012). This circular and resource-efficient economy would be a "resilient economy" which "should be achieved in a socially inclusive and responsible way" (European Commission, 2012).

The Circular Economy

According to an ING report on The Circular Economy, the world is becoming more populous and inhabited by richer people (ING, 2015). In 2015, the world population was 7.7 billion and by 2050 that figure is set to rise to 9.5 billion. For the year 2015, 54% (4.2 billion) of the world's population lived in cities. By 2050, the value will rise to 66% (6.3 billion). The middle class in 2015 was 23% (1.8 billion) of the world population. By 2050, that figure will be 52% (4.9 billion). The Dutch bank goes on to report:

> Global consumption currently needs 1,5 planet earths to sustain itself and this will increase with the rising middle class. If everybody in the world consumes at US level the world needs 4 planet earths. Clearly, the 'take, make and dispose' model in its current form is not sustainable in the long run (ING, 2015).

How can this challenge of unsustainability be addressed? Unlike the linear economy, the circular economy creates new ways of production:

1. Circular business models incorporate multiple principles around value creation. More than just financial values, they embrace environmental and social business values. These business models are focused around creating impact.

2. The supply chains of companies with circular business models

"often co-operate beyond traditional buyer supplier relationship that characterize linear supply chains" (ING, 2015). What they do instead is to operate in networks: companies and institutions strongly collaborate and co-create.

3. New markets are created where consumers interact with other consumers (C2C) and in which entities act as both manufacturer as well as consumer (C2B). As ING reports: "Money is the main, but not necessarily the sole, medium of exchange as goods or services are for example exchanged against energy, time or waste"(ING, 2015).

4. In linear modes of production, ownership is part of the logic of delivery. In the circular economy, access to a service is more important than product ownership.

5. Cost benefit analysis is the metric used to measure success in linear modes of production. However, in the circular economy non-financial values are incorporated along with financial values for all the stakeholders involved along with society at large.

This is accomplished by:
- Using fully renewable, recyclable or biodegradable resource inputs
- Extending the product life cycle
- Offering a product as a service
- Using sharing platforms to promote collaborative consumption
- The recovery of resources at the end of a product life cycle

ING elucidates the concept of the circular economy through its origins as an inspiration from nature. The bank writes, "In nature waste does not exist, there is no landfill as materials flow constantly in circles. Things grow, die at some point and become nutrients for other life. This is however not a perpetuum mobile: a system that keeps functioning in itself and creates energy out of nothing. To keep this cycle going, it needs energy which is provided by the sun" (ING, 2015). It is important to note that the circular economy is much more than just recycling. Recycling a computer, for example, is an exercise in diminishing returns. The value of the raw materials in a $1200 computer is roughly $9. When recycled, ING claims: "if the computer is 100% recycled less than 1 % of the value can be recovered" (ING, 2015). The activities of reuse, maintenance, and repair have the most potential. ING gives an example:

> Think of a large five star hotel in which every room needs an iron. After three years the hotel manager might decide to replace all its irons to keep up with the latest products. If the irons are recycled its materials can partly be used to make new ones. While this is far better than simply ditching the old irons even more value is created if the irons are reused. Think of a two star hotel that does not need its guests to use the latest models. If the five star hotel sells its irons to a two star hotel the product life is increased and much more value is created. The same applies to maintenance and repair activities. Through proper maintenance and repair products can be used longer. Therefore reuse, maintenance and

repair activities have the highest circular potential in many supply chains (ING, 2015).

New business models for the supply chain and value chain open up a gamut of economic opportunities that can stimulate the growth of economies through the behavior of individuals and business.

Environmental Rights

Environmental rights are human rights. Everyone in society deserves to live in a pollution free environment, be given access to the information and data about their environment, participate in decision-making about their environment, and have access to justice with respect to their environment.

These rights have been on the agenda since the 1970s, for example, "the 1972 Stockholm Declaration of the United Nations Conference on the Human Environment and the link between natural environments and the enjoyment of fundamental human rights" (Pederson, 2010). Pederson explains: The European Court For Human Rights, more recently, has set a precedent for resting the obligation for risk factors from pollution of the environment adversely affecting individual's "private and family life" on public authorities (Pederson, 2010).

The 1998 Aarhus Convention put forth a tripartite decree on

environmental rights that touches on environmental information, public participation, and decisions affecting the environment.

Robust Design With Taguchi Methods

The history of the advancement of societies, especially those of Western countries and those in Asia, tells the story of the analytical mind as the primary resource. As this author mentioned earlier, advances in health have, no doubt, been driven by applied mathematics: for example, the use of statistics in health and human services. In quality engineering, the Taguchi Methods, developed by Genichi Taguchi, uses concepts from robust design: "to design products or processes which are robust, i.e., insensitive to the effects of noise sources as intended under a wide range of conditions" (Ben-Gal et al., 2007). The authors write in *Robust eco-design: A new application for air quality engineering*: "the principles of robust design have been widely applied to diverse areas, such as the design of VLSIs (Very-large-scale integration), optimization of communication networks, development of electronic circuits, laser engraving of photo masks, cash-flow optimization in banking, government policy making, and runway utilization improvement at airports" (Ben-Gal et al., 2007).

With robust design, the principles to consider are controllable factors and noise factors. Controllable factors—for example, the physical dimensions of an object like a stack—are called the design parameters. These are selected by the designer. The noise factors are those not selected by the designer: for example, "temperature, wind velocity and other atmospheric conditions" (Ben-Gal, et al., 2007). These uncontrollable noise factors "are the source of variability in the system" (Ben-Gal, et al., 2007). The act of experimenting with these two factors lead to solutions that address problems of robustness in an analytical way. The authors write, "A common practice in robust design methods is to evaluate different settings of the controllable factors via experimentation, while observing their interactions with the noise factors" (Ben-Gal, et al, 2007).

This component of the applied scientific development of Western and Asian societies is key to a process that encourages trial, error, and failure which lead to insight, innovation, and invention. Policy-making can use Taguchi methods in its approach to solving the policy issues with respect to the environment, society, and economy: an approach utilizing the principles of sustainability in tandem as a guiding mechanism.

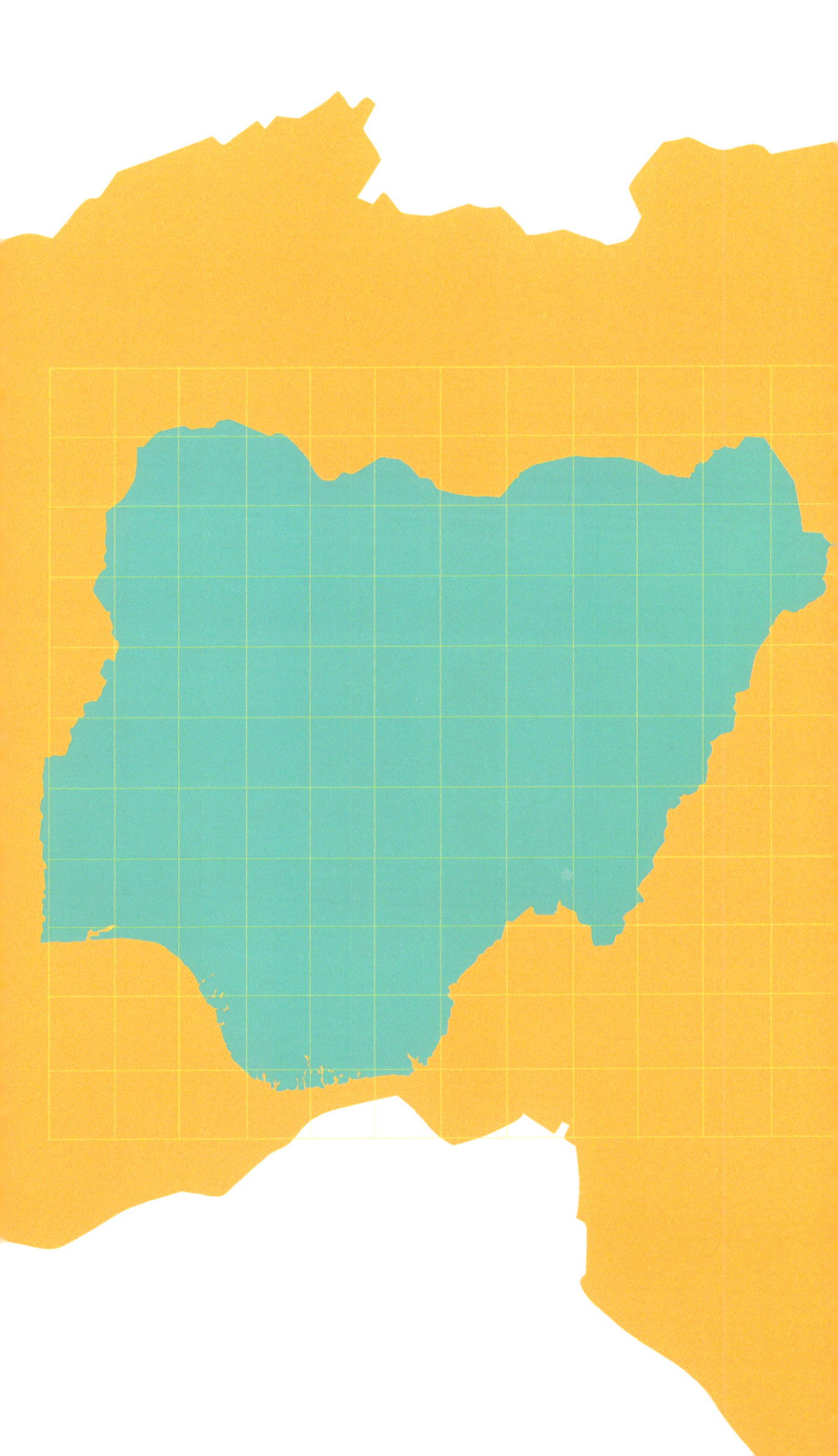

03
The Stakeholders

Local, State, and Federal Government

At its lowest level of government, Nigeria is comprised of 774 Local Government Areas (LGAs). The largest number of LGAs is in Kano. It has 44 LGAs. Bayelsa State has the fewest LGAs. It has 9. The Federal Capital Territory of Abuja has 6 LGAs. Any socio-economic transformation such as Agenda 2063—the shared framework for inclusive growth and sustainable development for Africa—would need to have success at the level of the LGA. This presents opportunities for policymakers to reach desired outcomes within smaller communities (LGAs) that have impact at the next level of government which is the State.

Nigeria is comprised of 36 states and 1 territory. They are: the Federal Capital Territory, Abia, Adamawa, Akwa Ibom, Anambra, Bauchi, Bayelsa, Benue, Borno, Cross River, Delta, Ebonyi, Edo, Ekiti, Enugu, Gombe, Imo, Jigawa, Kaduna, Kano, Katsina, Kebbi, Kogi, Kwara, Lagos, Nasarawa, Niger, Ogun, Ondo, Osun, Oyo, Plateau, Rivers, Sokoto, Taraba, Yobe, and Zamfara.

The federal government is composed of three distinct branches that check and balance each other similar to the government of the United States. These branches are the legislative, executive and judicial. Their powers are vested by the Constitution of Nigeria through the National Assembly, the President, and the federal courts, including the Supreme Court, respectively. Nigeria is a federal republic. The president holds and exercises executive power as the head of state, the head of government, and the head of a multi-party system. Politics in Nigeria takes place within a framework of a federal, presidential, representative democratic republic. Power is exercised in this republic by the government. Legislative power is held by the real government and the House of Representatives and the Senate—the two chambers of the legislature. These two houses, known as the National Assembly, are the law-making body of the nation. They serve as a check on the executive branch of government. The Supreme Court, the highest court in the nation, also acts within the separation of powers through checks and balances (CIA, 2018).

The commingling of policies that address the socio-economic development of Nigeria interacts with all these components of government at their respective levels. Policy at the level of the state affects the LGAs of that state, which can also be contested in the judicial branch and amended in the legislative branch. The president can also effect change through policy decisions exercised from the executive branch of government. The areas of accountability for sustainable development and growth permeates government. As a representative democratic republic, addressing systemic problems through socio-economic policies that affect change can happen through grassroots community organizing at the level of the LGAs. This can be achieved through bottom-up pressure on government by the self-organization of citizens within a community, and society at large. Concurrently, top-down leadership can also affect policy through the raising of issues, debates, and negotiated agreements for informed socio-economic development—informed by robustness with analytical models

—within the halls of the legislative and executive branches (Ben-Gal, et al., 2007).

Africa

The continent of Africa is composed of 54 fully recognised sovereign states. Nigeria has the largest population in Africa. The continent as a whole has 1.2 billion people as of 2016 and it accounts for about 16% of the global human population with a median age of 19.7 years(Janneh, 2012). In comparison, the worldwide median age is over 30 years(Ritchie and Roser, 2019). The majority of the stakeholders for Africa are the youth of the continent. They, however, face a crisis especially in sub-Saharan Africa: the learning crisis. According to the World Economic Forum, "88% of all children and adolescents in sub-Saharan Africa will not be able to read proficiently by the time they are of age to complete primary and lower secondary education" (Ifedi, 2018). The acuteness of such a crisis cannot be overstated. Although enrolment for primary school has increased from 60% to 80% over the past 20 years, the World Economic Forum reports: "on average less than 20% of primary school students in the region pass the minimum level of proficiency in reading and mathematics, compared to more than 50% of students in Latin America and even higher numbers in East Asia" (Ifedi, 2018). Furthermore, by 2055, Africa will have 1 billion children. The continent will be home to an estimated 40% of children in the world. In Africa, there's a great divide in education for the haves and the have-nots. The World Economic Forum writes: "Unless we can identify ways to accelerate learning for those currently left behind, many individuals and countries across the region will likely find themselves unable to benefit from the Fourth Industrial Revolution" (Ifedi, 2018). It is imperative that the stakeholders, the youth of Africa, have the skills necessary to chart a course that dramatically transforms their socio-economic reality by dealing with the challenges it faces, such as extreme poverty.

Humanity

In the seminal book, *The Limits To Growth; A Report for the Club of Rome's Project on the Predicament of Mankind*, the authors seek to investigate five major areas of concern, or trends: accelerating industrialization, rapid population growth, widespread malnutrition, depletion of nonrenewable resources, and a deteriorating environment (Meadows, et al., 1972). The authors argue that these trends are interconnected in several ways and their time scale can be measured not in mere months or years, as they argue in 1972, but "measured in decades or centuries". They present a model, a way of knowing, that seeks to "understand the causes of these trends, their interrelationships, and their implications as much as one hundred years in the future" (Meadows, et al., 1972). Their model for unpacking the future is mathematical and makes use of dynamically interacting variables such as population, food production, and pollution. These elements are not independent, but are interconnected, influence, and are influenced by each other in the real world. The mathematical nature of the authors' model reveal "implications for the future behavior of the world system" and "can be traced without error by a computer, no matter how complicated they become" (Meadows, et al., 1972). The use of a scientific approach, a mathematical model, is not done to give a complete technical assessment but "on what it tells us about the world. We have used a computer as a tool to aid our own understanding of the causes and consequences" (Meadows, et al., 1972). The authors come to this prescient conclusion at the state of Humanity in the World System:

> If the present growth trends in world population, industrialization, pollution, food production, and resource depletion continue unchanged, the limits to growth on this planet will be reached sometime within the next one hundred years. The most probable result will be a rather sudden and uncontrollable decline in both population and industrial capacity (Meadows et al., 1972).

The five major trends as the authors point out are all increasing exponentially. The question it raises is: if these dynamic, interconnected, and interrelated trends are not brought under control, what will the consequences for humanity be (Meadows et al., 1972)?

Nature

Fueled by the sun, nature creates interdependent, complex open systems with richness in diversity. It necessarily implies sustainability. On the other hand, industrialized society operates under the take, make, waste linear paradigm. In nature, waste is food. Natural complexity is reduced in industrialized society (William McDonough Architects, 1992). The challenge for humanity is to develop systems that integrate with the natural context.

An interaction between nature and humanity where nature itself is a stakeholder and has rights, just as persons. Concurrent to the natural rights of persons, there needs to be rights for nature to co-exist in a harmonious, sustaining condition with humanity (William McDonough Architects, 1992).

04
Principles for Sustainability

The Hannover Principles are a set of edicts that informed the designers in the international competition of EXPO 2000, the World's Fair in Hannover, Germany. The authors write: "The principles are to be considered by designers, planners, government officials and all involved in setting priorities for the built environment" (McDonough, 1992). Ultimately it serves as a foundation for sustainability in relation to the proposed systems and construction for the "city, its region, its global neighbors and partners in the world exposition" (McDononugh, 1992). If humankind is to continue to develop and improve its condition on this earth, "it is imperative to renew a commitment to living as part of the earth by understanding development and growth as processes which can be sustaining and restorative, not exploitive to impractical limits" (McDonough, 1992). The aim is to meet the needs and aspirations of the present without compromising the ability for an equally supportive and sustaining future:

THE HANNOVER PRINCIPLES

1. Insist on rights of humanity and nature to co-exist in a healthy, supportive, diverse and sustainable condition.

2. Recognize interdependence. The elements of human design interact with and depend upon the natural world, with broad and diverse implications at every scale. Expand design considerations to recognizing even distant effects.

3. Respect relationships between spirit and matter. Consider all aspects of human settlement including community, dwelling, industry and trade in terms of existing and evolving connections between spiritual and material consciousness.

4. Accept responsibility for the consequences of design decisions upon human well-being, the viability of natural systems and their right to co-exist.

5. Create safe objects of long-term value. Do not burden future generations with requirements for maintenance or vigilant administration of potential danger due to the careless creation of products, processes or standards.

6. Eliminate the concept of waste. Evaluate and optimize the full life-cycle of products and processes, to approach the state of natural systems, in which there is no waste.

7. Rely on natural energy flows. Human designs should, like the living world, derive their creative forces from perpetual solar income. Incorporate this energy efficiently and safely for responsible use.

8. Understand the limitations of design. No human creation lasts forever and design does not solve all problems. Those who create and plan should practice humility in the face of nature. Treat nature as a model and mentor, not as an inconvenience to be evaded or controlled.

9. Seek constant improvement by the sharing of knowledge. Encourage direct and open communication between colleagues, patrons, manufacturers and users to link long term sustainable considerations with ethical responsibility, and re-establish the integral relationship between natural processes and human activity (McDonough, 1992).

05
Systems Thinking for Systemic Problems

The problems Nigeria faces are systemic. They can be characterized as such because of the following reasons: problems are not merely isolated, for example corruption, or a lack of infrastructure. They're holistic in nature, dynamic, interdependent, and interconnected. The education system in Nigeria, for example, is interconnected with its economic system. They're mere parts in a larger system, a whole: the Nigeria System, a sovereign nation-state. An analogy of how systems work holistically, as wholes, Draper Kauffman writes:

> ...dividing the cow in half does not give you two smaller cows. You may end up with a lot of hamburger, but the essential nature of "cow"—a living system capable, among other things, of turning grass into milk—then would be lost. This is what we mean when we say a system functions as a "whole". Its behavior depends on its entire structure and not just on adding up the behavior of its different pieces (Kauffman, 1980).

It is with this spirit that it is said, for example, that the cow itself is a system, a living system within which there are other systems at play: the system boundary of its skin, interconnected with a natural (or industrial) farming system that is maintained and benefits from the ecosystem of solar energy and soil nutrients for grass to grow. However, when the cow is dismembered, it briefly stops being a system, it becomes disconnected and is a stagnant non-dynamic heap (Acaroglu, 2017). Leyla Acaroglu writes: "Under new conditions, it will enter into the industrial food production system, decompose into the natural system providing nutrients back to nature, or pass through a digestive system and contribute to that system's own function" (Acaroglu, 2017). The crux of the issue is that systems need to be defined in terms of their interrelationships and their functionality or potential (Acaroglu, 2017). In many respects, once a part of the system is taken away it stops functioning. If the wheels of a car are removed, or a vital organ from a body, the system ceases to work. Acaroglu writes, "one of the best examples of interactive systems design is nature—it is composed of many individual parts working together to create the dynamic whole that is the planet" (Acaroglu, 2017).

It is with this knowledge of the interconnectedness of Nigeria to a larger system, Africa as a whole, and to an even larger system, the world system that this author sees the potential of dynamic interrelationships that have impact based on intentions and choices that are both good and bad. The unintended consequences, for example of oil extraction, creates environmental disasters like Ogoniland, a mono economy tethered to the fluctuations of the price of oil in global markets creating recession, unemployment, crime, terrorism, corruption, disenfranchisement, etc. On the other hand, it makes Nigeria's economy the largest in Africa. There can be positive systems change fighting the less equitable aspects that interrelate to wreck the society from the quality of its air, which affects all in the society, to the development of the robustness of its infrastructure by potentially creating positive feedback loops into the rest of the country—here this author is thinking of the local development and private partnership for the development of the Egina Oil Field. Ultimately, what should be sought after with robust design and closed loop feedback systems and open systems in general are good outcomes.

The impact the Nigeria System needs to have starts at the beginning of all its productions, right from the start with insights from the dynamic and interrelating parts enhanced and reinforced by positive feedback loops. The latter will get disturbances, or negative feedback, but through a policy of continual energy invested to steer toward good robust outcomes, the insights gained will lead to circular outcomes driving a transformation of its socio-economic reality.

Coordination & Collaboration

Cooperation & Deliberation

06
Life-Cycle Analysis

In *The Hannover Principles: Design For Sustainability*, McDonough gathers together and frames the attitude, work, and aspirations of life-cycle analysis. He mentions the importance of life-cycle analysis for all materials and processes. In the case of Nigeria, it is no less both as well. The analysis is a process of assessing the "energy use and environmental impact of the entire life cycle of the product, process, or activity" (McDonough, 1992). For McDonough, it must be "catalogued and analyzed, encompassing extraction and processing of raw materials, manufacturing, transportation and maintenance, recycling, and return to the environment" (McDonough, 1992).

The goal of this thinking should be circularity, by thinking of material and form decisions impacting the natural world, alongside processes which involve the human value chain and the supply chain taken together as interconnected and interdependent. The material extraction of oil and gas needs to be seen within a larger context in the Nigeria System. How does the extraction affect the environment, the society, and the economy? In what ways can Nigeria contribute to The Circular Economy where waste, for example, can be exchanged for energy, or money? How can the benefits from oil extraction, for example infrastructure know-how, affect the transportation network of the country and the distribution of energy to a population of 190.9 million people? What does a robust and sustainable network of transport encompassing land, air, and water powered by energy affect the environment, the society, the economy? What makes it sustainable? When the finite resource of fossil fuel has reached depletion, what sources of revenue will exist for the country? How will it affect the economy, unemployment, crime, health and human services, infrastructure etc? The end-of-life impacts need to be assessed for all products, activities and processes in the Nigeria System. As Acaroglu writes: "What we have discovered from years of scientific explorations of impacts is that they are often not what you may initially think they are" (Acaroglu, 2018)!

As this author mentioned in the chapter on Systems Thinking, there are impacts to products, activities, and processes. One merely thinks of the impact the automobile had on American society, indeed on the world, from the development of the assembly line for manufacturing with interchangeable parts, the Interstate Highway System, the growth of suburbia, to greenhouse gas emissions. The relationships within a complex network of nodes and vertices in the product, process, and activities interact with the bigger system. Value creation needs to be thought of in a holistic way. The entire Nigeria System needs to be taken into consideration in terms of its accountability, values, ethics, and integrity in terms of its matrix for decision-making at the various levels and branches of government, the behavior of the citizen, indeed for policy-making with a holistic view toward the nation-state, Africa, and its global neighbors. Ultimately, the goal should be to design a regenerative, sustainable, circular system that is infinite. The nation cannot deflect the responsibility for the beginning and end-of-life for products, processes, and activities that affect its environment, society, and economy which create productions that interact with larger systems in the global order. In systems thinking, it is often said that the smallest part of a system has the biggest potential for change. Nigeria can start to build solutions for a positive future for not only itself, but for its global neighbors.

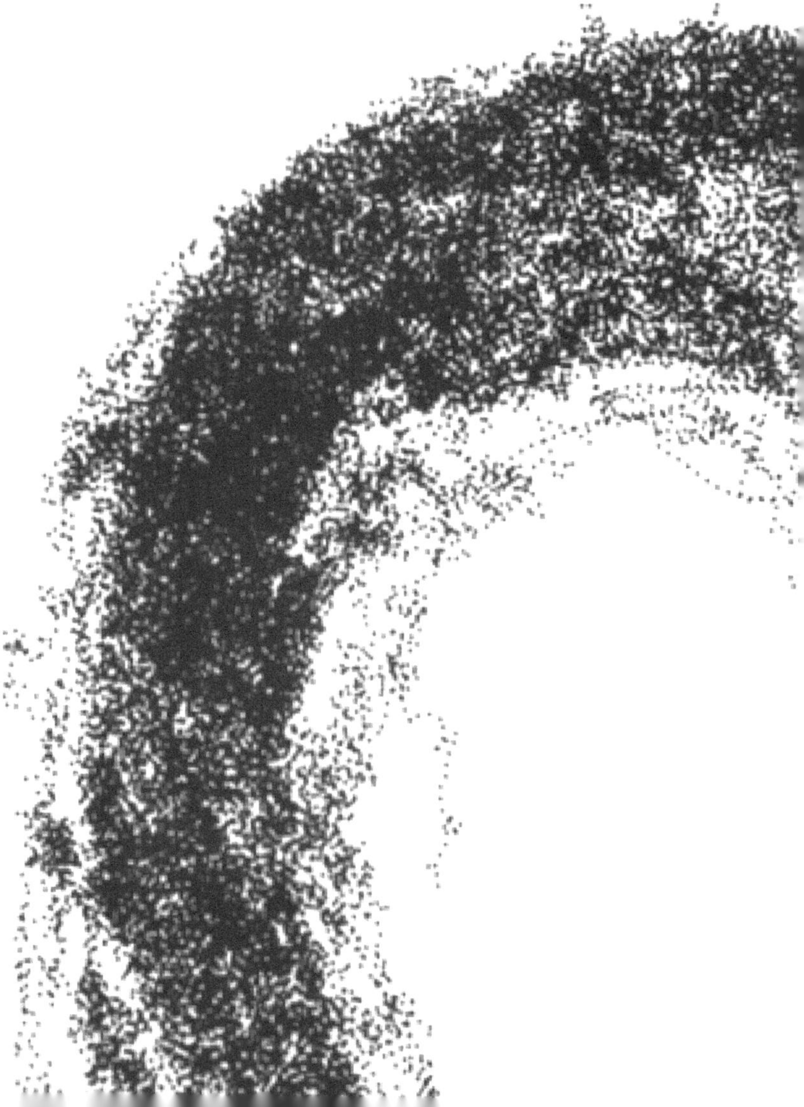

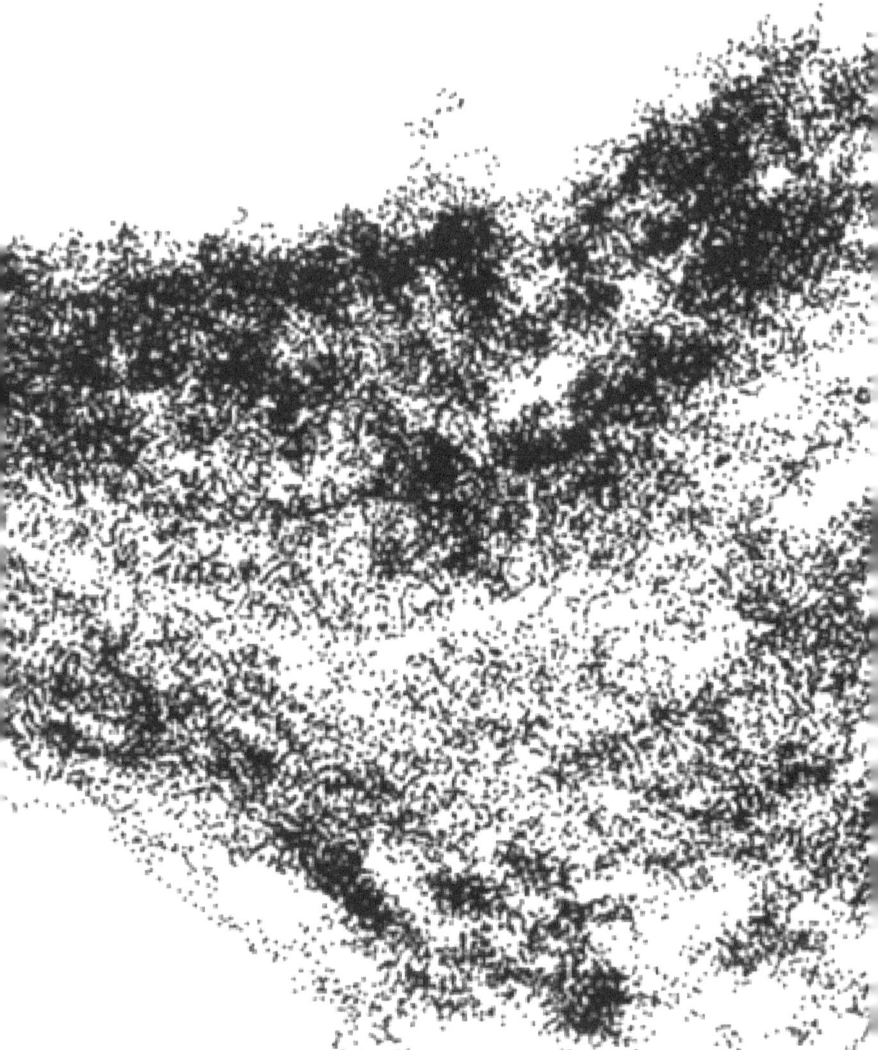

07
Collective Intelligence

Learning From Nature: Swarm Intelligence

The history of humankind has been a transformation of her environment. The spiritual life and civic life of the ancient Egyptians centered around the Nile river Valley: its symbol, the lotus flower, represented for the ancient Egyptians the regeneration of life. Humankind has continually looked to nature for answers to problems. It is in nature we find everything that we need to live as fully as possible. It gives us the five ancient forces still applicable today: earth, air, water, fire, spirit. The complexity of these forces brings a diversity to the natural world that should give any student of science, mathematics, art, design, and engineering pause. In nature, we find fractal geometry which gives the sublimity of the whole contained within the part recurring to infinity. The earth, as context and material, holds nutrients that form part of our ecology that affects the growth of rainforests where we find plants that cure disease. Indeed, nature is our teacher, provider, mentor through the ages of humankind and will continue to be so.

At the vanguard of research into artificial intelligence at the most distinguished universities, the neural network of the brain isn't the only area of concern for those building robots and autonomous systems, but also simpler entities—with the biological principles of self-assembly and self-organization—in nature capable of solving complex problems in ever changing dynamic environments. These principles turn individual behavior, which might seem random, toward emergent global collective order from the complexity of the stochastic. Klaus Shwab—executive director and founder of The World Economic Forum—predicts a "fusing" together of "the physical, digital and biological worlds, impacting all disciplines, economies and industries, and even challenging ideas about what it means to be human" (The World Economic Forum, n.d.). This author adds all societies to the mix which will be upended in the near future because of this fusion.

In a society such as Nigeria, a place that never realized industrialization, there exists a potential to create a new future, a future of growth and complete transformation if the challenges facing the country can be approached through an understanding of its unique advantage in Africa, its global relationship with its neighbors, and the development of these strengths through analytical and applied scientific decision making. Nigeria has institutions of researchers such as the Nigerian Mathematical Society, researchers who publish academic papers—for example, *A Note On The Replenishment Of Infrastructure*—building models of dynamic systems. It behooves policymakers to address the energy crisis in Nigeria, for example, through mathematical models and simulations of dynamic and open systems with interdependent variables to aid in the planning of energy policy—continuous energy distribution and delivery through a variety of inputs. Over the past sixty years, Nigeria's energy production has exponentially decayed. The country needs different thinking around similar policy issues.

Globalization 4.0, or The Fourth Industrial Revolution, will require new skills for the world population. Nigeria and its citizens will not be exempt. Education is critical to the success of the youth and the country. Bridge International Academies is an innovative leader in education across Africa and India. Since 2009, their model has empowered and reached 500,000 children through several hundreds of schools. The innovative venture began with the premise of solving an "intractable problem; hundreds of millions of children worldwide who do not have access to schools that empower and inspire them" (Bridge International Academies, n.d.). Bridge addresses the problem of the shortage of learning by aiding and boosting government schools whilst running "complementary affordable schools" (Bridge International Academies, n.d.).

Their simple belief: "every child has the right to education" (Bridge International Academies, n.d.). This propels Bridge to work hand in hand with key stakeholders: "governments, communities, teachers and parents to improve or deliver high quality nurseries and primary schools in underserved areas" (Bridge International Academies, n.d.).

Their approach is scientific. They're data driven and work with empirical evidence. Their education delivery system, or education as a service, "adapts to the needs of individual governments. We have re-engineered every part of the education system, from teacher training and support, to lesson delivery, construction, and financial administration; making our academies as effective and affordable as possible" (Bridge International Academies, n.d.).

Bridge works in four states in Nigeria: Lagos, Osun, Edo, and Borno States. As Bridge writes on its website: "Our work in Nigeria gives us the potential to positively impact the lives of millions of children. We're developing a range of partnerships to help improve education outcomes" (Bridge International Academies, n.d.). They go on to mention their "partnership model in collaboration with the Nigerian Stock Exchange and the Borno State Government" (Bridge International Academies, n.d.).

Nigeria is a place of immense complexity. Its diversity of languages, cultures, ethnic groups, education levels, geography, and ecologies present heterogeneity as a priori. Fundamentally, the country is an open system. This brings the promise of equifinality. However, there are secondary forces which can be modeled to show its effect on policymaking. These forces exhibit biomimetic characteristics: self-assembly and self-organization.

Self-assembly are processes that display collective order from dynamic small-scale interactions. These processes are spontaneous and are at a state of equilibrium. The interactions, however, are numerous among lower level components in the absence of global information. Ultimately, the low level components are a set encoded with specific and directional information that interact with other components (Halley and Winkler, 2008).

The critical points here are:

1. The spontaneous processes and the interactions among lower level components in the absence of global information.

2. A dynamic and engaged community—a Local Government Area (LGA) as a lower level component of governance in this biomi-

metic framework—can have numerous interactions amongst its constituents to present issues, positions, arguments, evolution of thought, agreements to act or transact around policies like education, economy, environment, governance, crime and terrorism, infrastructure, unemployment, gender equality, etc.

3. This would animate civic life and would be bottom-up community organizing. Data could also be captured through surveys on mobile devices and computers to help policy makers in leadership positions at the state level: a mix of bottom-up and top-down.

The biological principle of self-organization in organisms puts forth templates and blueprints that when utilized, as was mentioned earlier, inform scientific research on intelligence. More specifically, collective intelligence that emerges from the whole. For example, in a colony a single insect is not able to discover by itself an efficient solution to a colony problem; however, through stigmergy the society to which the insect belongs finds "as a whole" a solution very easily. In *The Biological Principles Of Swarm Intelligence*, the researchers call this display of collective will, "organization without an organizer" (Garnier, et al., 2007). It is important to note that the members of these social societies "only deal with partial and noisy information about their environment" (Garnier, et al., 2007). Their environment is in constant flux and they're capable of coping with uncertain situations; yet they find solutions to complex problems. The researchers write: "Implementations in artificial systems of this swarm intelligence logic are nowadays numerous: discrete optimization (Dorigo, et al. 1996, 1999), graph partitioning (Kuntz, et al.1999), task allocation (Campos, et al. 2000; Krieger, et al. 2000), object clustering and sorting (Melhuish, et al. 2001; Wilson, et al. 2004), collective decision making" (Garnier, et al. 2005), and so on. How does this work? What are the principles that can inform change for civil society broadly and Nigeria more specifically from a policy perspective?

The major concepts which underpin swarm intelligence are "decentralization, stigmergy, self-organization, emergence, positive and negative feedbacks, fluctuations, bifurcations. It also highlights the nature of the relation between the behavior of the individual and the behavior of the group" (Garnier, et al., 2007). Each of these concepts can be explored in more detail elsewhere. However, keeping the idea of components and its capacity as a tool for understanding relationships (environment and community). Swarm intelligence can be categorized based on the interplay of four behavioral components: coordination, cooperation, collaboration, and deliberation.

1. Coordination occurs because of the appropriate organization in space and time of the tasks required to solve a specific problem. Coordination is also involved in the exploitation of sources for sustenance by building a trail network that spatially organizes the behavior between their domain and one or more sources of sustenance (Garnier, et al., 2007).

2. Cooperation occurs when individuals "achieve together a task that could not be done by a single one" (Garnier, et al.,2007). The individuals together must combine their efforts in order to be

successful at solving a problem that goes beyond their individual abilities. In ants, for example, it could be the cooperative transport of prey: "a very efficient way to bring back food to the nest" (Garnier, et al., 2007). The researchers add: "it was reported that ants engaged in the cooperative transport of a prey can hold at least ten times more weight than did solitary transporters" (Garnier, et al., 2007).

3. Collaboration occurs when different activities are "performed simultaneously by groups of specialized individuals" (Garnier, et al., 2007).

4. Deliberation occurs because of mechanisms which present the community with several opportunities. The authors write, "these mechanisms result in a collective choice for at least one of the opportunities" (Garnier, et al., 2007). For example, ants of the species Lasius niger "have discovered several food sources with different qualities or richness, or several paths that lead to a food source, they generally select only one of the different opportunities" (Garnier, et al., 2007). The deliberation is driven by the competition between trails that lead to each opportunity. The richer and shorter path toward the source of sustenance usually wins the competition (Garnier, et al., 2007).

A note about specialization: The researchers write, it "can rely on a pure behavioral differentiation" (Garnier, et al., 2007). For example, the age of the individuals.

The information processing capabilities of the community occur along two main axes through the continuous flux of interactions between members of the community: coordination and collaboration; cooperation and deliberation. Coordination and collaboration "shape the spatial, temporal and social structures that result from" the work of the community (Garnier, et al., 2007). In other words, the function of coordination is to regulate the spatio-temporal density of individuals while collaboration functions by regulating the allocation of the activities of individuals. Cooperation and deliberation function by providing tools for the community to address its environmental challenges. Deliberation functions support decision making of the community. Cooperation functions address the limits of the individual by presenting mechanisms that go beyond her limitations.

Taken together, the four functions of self-organization, "organization without an organizer", produce solutions to the community's problems (Garnier, et al., 2007. As the researchers point out, it "may give the impression that the colony as a whole plans its work to achieve its objectives" (Garnier, et al., 2007). They go on to note: these interacting behavioral components occur among the members of the community and between them and their environment. In terms of the ant colony example, the researchers write: "Because the colony and its environment permanently evolve in time, they can be considered as coupled dynamic systems" (Garnier, et al., 2007).

Not only are communities that exhibit these interacting behaviors dynamic, they are also adaptive: they counterbalance the effects of "a potentially harmful perturbation" by modifying their behavior

(Garnier et al., 2007). The collective adaptation only occurs because of the modulation of individual behavior. The researchers write, the "individual is able to sense the variation thanks to local cues it slightly modifies its behavior in response" (Garnier et al., 2007). Furthermore, behavioral modifications affect the interaction network, and thus "the global structure through a new balancing of positive and negative feedbacks" (Garnier, et al., 2007).

There are two factors which influence the community due to perturbations: "outer community" and "inner community" perturbations. For ants, we can substitute community with colony. The outer parameters come from outside the social structure of the community: for example, ecological parameters or its sustenance network parameters. "Inner community" factors are directly linked to the components of the community: for example, its population, the ratio of different sub-groups, learning, etc.

Positive feedback loops reinforce the successful achievement of a task for an individual in the community, and "may favor the future achievement of the same task" (Garnier, et al., 2007). As the researchers write, "a subtle network of interacting influences regulates individual behaviors" providing the community with a "real-time solution to a real-time problem" (Garnier et al., 2007). Competition and specialization are tools that influence the interaction of individuals within the community creating a division of labor in terms of task specialization. As the researchers write: "When the total workload is high, which is the case in a large colony, it is better to have specialized workers whose performance in task execution will be optimal instead of having generalist workers with a lower performance. On the contrary, when the total amount of work is small, which is the case in a small colony, it might be more relevant to have generalist workers" (Garnier, et al., 2007). This assures the optimal cost for workers by not having specialized workers, who would not work frequently (Garnier, et al., 2007).

The deliberation for a domain, a site for work, sustenance and living is based on "quorum sensing" by the individual recruitment behavior of scouts (Garnier, et al., 2007). Here the deliberation is a collective choice. Scouts that discover a suitable domain come back to the old domain and recruit a single domain-mate by leading them to the domain. The domain-mate assesses by herself the qualities of the potential domain before recruiting a further domain-mate by leading her own run to the source (a tandem run). The quality of the domain affects the duration of assessment: a better domain is assessed more quickly. This "then induces a traffic flow which grows more rapidly" (Garnier, et al., 2007). When a quorum is reached—"the minimum number of individuals that must be present in order for a decision to be taken—the recruitment behavior turns from tandem runs (one domain-mate leading another domain-mate) to direct transport by carrying passive individuals to the new domain (Garnier, et al., 2007). "This recruitment by transport is three times faster than recruitment by tandem runs"(Pratt, et al., 2002). The amplification of the initial choice helps reach the quorum faster and other potential domains don't reach their quorum. This mechanism of amplification can also be modulated to adapt the decision making process of the colony to different environmental conditions" (Garnier, et al., 2007). This author adds economic and societal conditions as elements bounded by environment.

These behavioral principles as interactions, the activities of community, should be amplified continuously within, between, among communities and their environments as dynamic open systems. This author believes Nigeria has the potential to use these innovative principles of organic intelligence—at the vanguard of artificial systems research—to solve its most intractable and systemic problems with robustness. Nigerians have the capacity to hustle via self-organization—organization without an organizer. The spontaneous process of achieving together order at the global level (the nation): that is to say, even in the absence of complete information of a blueprint within their respective communities (LGAs and villages). This can be achieved from the urban (Lagos) to the rural (a single village): "the whole" (nation) contained within "the part" (individual community).

Connected Things: The Power of Networks

In *New Rules For The New Economy*, Kevin Kelly lays out a future that embraces the metaphor of the net: it has no center, no certainty; it is an "indefinite web of causes". As an archetype, it "represents all circuits, all intelligence, all communications, all democracy, all families, all large systems, almost all that we find interesting and important" (Kelly, 1998). The author, founding executive editor of *Wired* magazine, proclaims the net as our future. The most far reaching of human endeavors to date has been the "weaving together of our lives, minds, and artifacts" into what he calls "a global scale network", due in no small part to both the silicon chip and the silicate glass fiber (Kelly, 1998). This bringing together has unleashed a powerful and pervasive net. Kelly emphasizes, "As this grand net spreads, an animated swarm is reticulating the surface of the planet. We are clothing the globe with a network society" (Kelly, 1998).

Understanding how networks work will be key to understanding how the economy works, its logic defined by nodes and connections. These are two ingredients with diverging characteristics: the size of the nodes are getting smaller "while the quantity and quality of the connections are exploding" (Kelly, 1998). As the size of a single chip with transistors shrinks to the nanoscale, the price exponentially decreases. Kelly illustrates this point: "In 1950 a transistor cost five dollars. Today it costs one hundredth of a cent" (Kelly, 1998). He goes even farther by predicting that a "chip with a billion transistors will eventually cost only a few cents" (Kelly, 1998).

The cheapness and size of chips means they can go into everything everywhere. In 1998, there were already 6 billion non-computer chips "pulsating in the world" (Kelly, 1998). Their numbers are increasing exponentially. He writes: "You already have a non-PC chip embedded in your car and stereo and rice cooker and phone. These chips are dumb chips, with limited ambitions. A chip in your car's brakes doesn't have to do floating-point math, spreadsheets, or video processing; it only needs to brake like a bulldog" (Kelly, 1998). He is writing before the emergence of the smartphone.

The extremely low price of these chips means they can be stamped out in large quantities. These dumb "jelly bean chips" are "invading the world far faster than PCs did" (Kelly, 1998). He predicts in 1998, "there'll be some 10 billion tiny grains of silicon chips embedded into our environment" (Kelly, 1998). Connecting the nodes of these dumb chips, one by one, and linking them together into a swarm: we create something more than dumb, we create intelligence, we gather data (Kelly, 1998). For example, "we can get real-time buying patterns that can manage inventory" (Kelly, 1998). In other words, when connected "into a swarm, small thoughts become smart" (Kelly, 1998).

The key point here is that when a small amount of data is transmitted and receives input from its environment, we change "an inert object into an animated node" (Kelly, 1998). It doesn't take sophisticated infrastructure to transmit the data of these "dumb bits". He writes:

> Stationary objects—parts of a building, tools on the factory floor, fixed cameras—are wired together. The nonstationary rest—that is, most manufactured objects—are linked by infrared and radio, creating a wireless web vastly larger than the wired web (Kelly, 1998).

These are the same frequencies that run TV remote controls (Kelly, 1998). Taken together, these connected things don't need to

Collective Intelligence

have individual sophistication: no need for artificial intelligence, speech recognition, machine learning etc. The connecting of these nodes are similar to how the world wide web creates intelligence "by connecting dumb personal computers. A personal computer is like a single brain neuron in a plastic box" (Kelly, 1998). Their power is in the linking together (Kelly, 1998). He points out how dumb cells in the "body work together in a swarm to produce incredibly smart immune system, a system so sophisticated we still do not comprehend it" (Kelly, 1998).

The ultimate aim of "swarm power is superior performance in a turbulent environment" (Kelly, 1998). He gives several examples of the use of swarm intelligence in business: from delivering wet cement to painting cars on a GM assembly line to railways employing swarm technology in Japan. However, he writes, "complete surrender to the bottom is not what embracing swarm is about" (Kelly, 1998). That is to say without some element of leadership and governance from the top, "bottom-up control will freeze when options are many" (Kelly, 1998). Without some element of minimal leadership, "the many at the bottom will become paralyzed with choices" (Kelly, 1998). On the other hand, Kelly writes: "We have spent centuries obsessed with the role of top-down governance. Its importance remains. But the great excitement of the new economy is that we have only begun to explore the power of the bottom, where peers holds [sic] sway" (Kelly 1998). He offers the proposition that there is far more gain "by pushing the boundaries of what can be done by the bottom than by focusing on what can be done at the top" (Kelly, 1998). The power of this century is the power of decentralized and autonomous networks (Kelly, 1998).

08
Framework

In 2016, Bloomberg reported Nigeria's population to be 182 million with more than half of the population under 30 years of age (Mbachu and Alake, 2016). The large number of youth in Nigeria is an asset because of the new approaches and ideas they bring to problem solving. Most of them are digital-native; thus, they are aware and open to a technological approach as a way for providing solutions to problems. Nigerians also have ingenuity. They find solutions to problems through inventiveness and hard work. In many fields, Nigerians—both inside and outside of the country—have distinguished themselves as top practitioners. The coming together of all of the above presents promise for realizing a new Nigeria: a framework for its future. The eight points below rely on a bottom up approach which incorporates citizen-to-government (C2G), business-to-government (B2G), consumer-to-consumer (C2C), consumer-to-business (C2B), and business-to-business (B2B) through the use of swarm intelligence:

1. Network Nigeria. Connect every citizen to a network infrastructure enabling them to learn together, work together, live together peacefully, and make decisions together with the use of data.

2. Use expertise. Determine expertise by allowing individuals to compete to accomplish tasks. Use winners of competitions to form groups of specialized individuals who work simultaneously to solve specific policy problems.

3. Design for robustness together. Create robust sustainable solutions that are long lasting and continually improve them through iterations.

4. Use speed. Use the shortest path in the network to facilitate the speed for action.

5. Work together. Accomplish with each other a task that cannot be done by a single individual.

6. Learn from others and use what works. Utilize the successes of others and their endeavors to enable more success.

7. Use data to select opportunities. Capture meaningful data on the environment, society, economy and use it as an opportunity to make sustainable policy decisions.

8. Choose one option together. Make a collective choice on the opportunity that solves a policy problem. Develop the opportunity until goals are successfully achieved. Repeat this process using data to address more areas for policy-making and improvements to the environment, society, and economy.

References

Acaroglu, L.(2017, September 13). Tools for Systems Thinkers: Getting into Systems Dynamics... and Bathtubs. Retrieved January 11, 2019, from https://medium.com/disruptive-design/tools-for-systems-thinkers-getting-into-systems-dynamics-and-bathtubs-1f961f7c4073

Acaroglu, L. (2018, January 21). Six Steps to Circular Systems Design – Disruptive Design –Medium. Retrieved January 11, 2019, from https://medium.com/disruptive-design/six-steps-to-circular-systems-design-1b0c8ae9f60e

Agenda 2063 (pp. 1-24, Rep.). (2015). African Union Commission.

Barzilay, E. J., Vandi, H., Binder, S., Udo, I., Ospina, M. L., Ihekweazu, C., & Bratton, S. (2018). Use of the Staged Development Tool for Assessing, Planning, and Measuring Progress in the Development of National Public Health Institutes. Health Security, 16(S1). doi:10.1089/hs.2018.0044

Ben-Gal, I., Katz, R., & Bukchin, Y. (2008). Robust eco-design: A new application for air quality engineering. IIE Transactions, 40(10), 907-918. doi:10.1080/07408170701775094

Dickson. (2018, October 11). IMF Tasks FG On Priority Spending Of Tax Revenues. Retrieved January 06, 2019, from https://leadership.ng/2018/10/11/imf-tasks-fg-on-priority-spending-of-tax-revenues-2/

Ekhosuehi, V. U., Iguodala, W. A., & Osagiede, A. A. (2016). A Note On The Replenishment Of Infrastructure. Journal of the Nigerian Mathematical Society, 35, 523-531. Retrieved January 16, 2019.

Environmental Survey of Ogoniland (pp. 1-19, Rep.). (2007). United Nations Environment Programme.

Garnier, S., Gautrais, J., & Theraulaz, G. (2007). The biological principles of swarm intelligence. Swarm Intelligence, 1(1), 3-31. doi:10.1007/s11721-007-0004-y

Green, C. (2008). *Thinking in Systems, A primer*, Donella H. Meadows. White River Junction, Vermont: Donella H. Meadows.

Halley, J. D., & Winkler, D. A. (2008). Consistent concepts of self-organization and self-assembly. Complexity, 14(2), 10-17. doi:10.1002/cplx.20235

Hannah Ritchie and Max Roser (2019) - "Age Structure". Published online at OurWorldInData.org. Retrieved August 05, 2022 from: 'https://ourworldindata.org/age-structure' [Online Resource]

Health And Human Services Statistics. (n.d.). Retrieved January 06, 2019, from https://www.proshareng.com/news/Nigeria Economy/Health-And-Human-Services-Statistics/14345

Human Development Reports. (n.d.). Retrieved January 06, 2019, from http://hdr.undp.org/en/countries/profiles/NGA

Human Development Reports. (n.d.). Retrieved January 06, 2019, from http://hdr.undp.org/en/countries/profiles/ZAF

Ifedi, A. (2018, October 19). How Nigeria is changing what we've learned about improving education.
Retrieved January 10, 2019, from https://www.weforum.org/agenda/2018/10/how-nigeria-is-changing-what-weve-learned-about-improving-education/

Kelly, K. (1998). *New rules for the new economy: 10 radical strategies for a connected world.* New York, NY: Penguin Books.

Manifesto For A Resource-Efficient Europe. (2012, December 17). Retrieved January 07, 2019, from http://europa.eu/rapid/press-release_MEMO-12-989_en.htm Memo Press Release.

McDonough, W., & Braungart, M. (2003). *The Hannover principles design for sustainability.* Charlottesville, VA: William Mc Donough Partners and McDonough Braungart Design Chemistry.

Meadows, D. H., Meadows, D. L., Randers, J., & Behrens, W. W. (1979). *The limits to growth: A report for the Club of Rome's project on the predicament of mankind.* New York: Universe Books.

Mike, U. (2018, December 6). Challenges in Nigeria and Solutions on How to Resolve Them. Retrieved January 06, 2019, from https://soapboxie.com/world-politics/challenges-in-Nigeria-and-solutions

Nigeria. (n.d.). Retrieved January 17, 2019, from https://www.bridgeinternationalacademies.com/where-we-work/nigeria/

Overview. (2018). Retrieved January 06, 2019, from https://www.worldbank.org/en/country/nigeria/overview

Pederson, O. (2010). A Bill of Rights, Environmental Rights and the UK Constitution. Public Law, n/a(2), 577-595, Retrieved August 08, 2022 from https://www.academia.edu/3649122/A_Bill_of_Rights_Environmental_Rights_and_the_UK_Constitution

Quote of the Day: John von Neumann. (2022). Retrieved August 5, 2022, from https://ricochet.com/569608/quote-of-the-day-john-von-neumann/

Rethinking finance in a circular economy a circular economy: Financial implications of circular business models (pp. 1-57, Working paper). (2015). ING Economics Department. ING Bank N.V. published this report solely for informational purposes only. It is not investment advice.

SDGs .:. Sustainable Development Knowledge Platform. (n.d.). Retrieved January 07, 2019, from https://sustainabledevelopment.un.org/sdgs

Soni, J., & Goodman, R. (2018). *A Mind at Play: How Claude Shannon Invented the Information Age* (Unabridged ed.). N/A, United States: Simon & Schuster.

The Establishment Act. (n.d.). Retrieved January 06, 2019, from https://efccnigeria.org/efcc/about-efcc/the-establishment-act

The Fourth Industrial Revolution, by Klaus Schwab. (n.d.). Retrieved January 12, 2019, from https://www.weforum.org/about/the-fourth-industrial-revolution-by-klaus-schwab

The World Factbook: Nigeria. (n.d.). Retrieved January 06, 2019, from https://www.cia.gov/library/publications/the-world-factbook/geos/print_ni.html

Top 10 Shocking Facts About Poverty in Nigeria. (2018, July 02). Retrieved January 06, 2019, from https://borgenproject.org/10-facts-about-poverty-in-nigeria/

Top 70 Wole Soyinka Quotes (2022 Update). (2022). Retrieved August 5, 2022, from https://quotefancy.com/wole-soyinka-quotes

Who we are. (n.d.). Retrieved January 17, 2019, from https://www.bridgeinternationalacademies.com/who-we-are/

CPSIA information can be obtained
at www.ICGtesting.com
Printed in the USA
LVHW010216010623
748611LV00013B/31